Releasing & Letting Go of Excess Baggage

The Interactive Workshop Journal

Part 2 of the
Shattered But Not Destroyed
Series

With
Dr. Patricia Logan-Miles

Releasing & Letting Go of Excess Baggage
The Interactive Workshop Journal
Part of the *Shattered But Not Destroyed* series
Copyright © 2015 by Dr. Patricia Logan-Miles

ISBN-13: 978-1523461875
ISBN-10: 152346187X

All rights reserved. No part of this book may be reproduced or transmitted in any form or by any means without written permission of the author.

SOV Books
Downey, California

Printed in the United States of America

Be sure to pick up a copy of

Part 1 of this series ...

Shattered But Not Destroyed

By Dr. Patricia Logan-Miles

Go to: Amazon Books Dr. Patricia Logan-Miles

Or write: drpatmiles@yahoo.com

The Flush Index

Introduction	1
Instruction # 1 – For Workshop Participants	3
Introduction # 2 – For Participants Working On Their Own	5
Baggage 1 -- Unforgiveness	11
Baggage 2 –- Living In The Past	23
Baggage 3 -- Guilt	35
Baggage 4 -- Self-Loathing	47
Baggage 5 -- Anger & Rage	59
The Prayer of Acceptance & Forgiveness	71
Your Progress Checklist	77
Contact Information	79

Welcome to the Releasing & Letting Go! Workshop!

We're glad you decided to join us!

Now, let's get ready to dive into the deepest parts of our souls, dispose of our excess baggage at the bottom of the ocean, never to remember it again.

Before you know it, you'll be swimming in the fresh, clean waters of your brand-new life!

Please turn off all cell phones and other devices and stay focused.

OK, here we go … Let's begin …

Introduction

Removing excess baggage from your soul may not be something you can do on your own.

The Flushing Process "gives permission" by your spoken word to the Lord to do this for you!

Luke 4.18 declares that the Lord is the one who opens prison doors and sets the captives free, not you!

It's all about you giving him *permission* to do so, not about you having to do it alone!

Here's a list of baggage we'll be dealing with ...

      Baggage 1 -- Unforgiveness

      Baggage 2 -- Living In The Past

      Baggage 3 -- Guilt

      Baggage 4 -- Self-Loathing

      Baggage 5 -- Anger / Rage

      The results will be wonderful!

Instruction # 1

Supplies You'll Need

1. A copy of the book ...

    Releasing & Letting Go of Excess Baggage

2. You may also want to purchase a copy of Dr. Pat's book -- **Shattered But Not Destroyed** – which describes the outrageous things that happened to her, and are the actual genesis of her current ministry!

2. Your Bible

3. A Pen

4. And a willing heart!

Instruction # 2

For Those Participating In The Workshop:

This fun, interactive journal has been included to assist you with this flushing process in caring, support-network environment.

1. If possible, read the baggage chapters in the *Releasing & Letting Go* book before coming to class and complete the baggage assignment in this journal.

2. This fun, interactive journal was designed to help you articulate in writing your grievances before the Lord.

3. After reading each baggage chapter, open your journal and partake of the vital, written exercises. Add additional sheets of paper if needed and staple them inside this journal.

4. After completing the written, Flushing Assignments, the class will turn to the back of this journal and read together and out loud *The Prayer of Acceptance & Deliverance,* after each chapter, signifying that you have flushed that particular piece of baggage.

    Each Assignment chapter has two contracts. Sign both copies.

5. Then sign the contract together with the class, before the Lord and your fellow, workshop participants.

6. Now cut out one of the contracts and leave the second copy in the book, as a reminder that you expelled that excess baggage on the date.

7. Tear up one copy ceremoniously and throw it away, never to be revisited ever again.

8. Repeat the above steps for each baggage chapter.

For Those Participating On Their Own:

Read one baggage chapter at a time in the *Releasing & Letting Go* book, starting with Baggage 1.

This fun, interactive journal was designed to help you articulate your grievances before the Lord.

After reading each baggage chapter, open your journal and partake of the vital, written exercises. Add additional sheets of paper if needed and staple them inside this journal. This journal will greatly assist you in the Flushing Process.

After completing the written, Flushing Assignment make an appointment with the Lord.

On The Day of The Appointment ...

1. Be sure that your notes on each baggage are clearly defined. State the reasons for your wounds

2. Turn off the TV and your cell phone

3. Close the curtains

4. Eat and drink ahead of time

5. Have *The Prayer of Acceptance and Deliverance* ready.

6. And get to a place where you can pray out loud.

7. Now, turn to the back of this book and read out loud *The Prayer of Acceptance & Deliverance*.

8. Each Assignment chapter has two contracts. Please sign both copies.

9. Sign both contracts before the Lord.

10. Now cut out one of the contracts out and leave the second copy in the book as a reminder that you expelled that excess baggage on that date.

11. Tear up one copy ceremoniously and throw it away, never to be revisited ever again.

12. Repeat the above steps for each baggage chapter.

Isaiah 61:1-3

The Spirit of the Lord GOD is upon me; because the LORD hath anointed me to preach good tidings unto the meek; he hath sent me to bind up the brokenhearted, to proclaim liberty to the captives, and the opening of the prison to them that are bound;

To proclaim the acceptable year of the LORD, and the day of vengeance of our God; to comfort all that mourn;

To appoint unto them that mourn in Zion, to give unto them beauty for ashes, the oil of joy for mourning, the garment of praise for the spirit of heaviness; that they might be called trees of righteousness, the planting of the LORD, that he might be glorified.

I THINK THAT YOU HAVE SOME SERIOUS FAITH ISSUES

Baggage 1
Unforgiveness

Baggage 1 -- Unforgiveness

This exercise deals with unforgiveness.

Write down the names of all those whom you've had a hard time forgiving

Briefly describe the events that caused you to fall into unforgiveness.

Continue on this page …

Concerning this matter, what would you like the Lord to do for you?

Before you let it go forever, is there anything else you'd like to tell the Lord?

Now, turn the page to review the contract.

Don't sign it until the class director says it's time to do so.

Read the Prayer of Acceptance and Deliverance with the class.

Then sign and date both contracts, promising to yourself and to the Lord that you'll never revisit these things again.

Cut out one of the contracts and throw it away – ceremoniously – to commemorate your Day of Deliverance.

If doing this on your own, read the Prayer of Acceptance and Deliverance at the back of this journal and repeat the steps above.

Congratulations on your new-found freedom from unforgiveness!

Releasing & Letting Go Contract

Unforgiveness

I, _____, promise my Lord and Savior, Jesus, that as of this date, _____,

I have willingly and deliberately released and let go of all unforgiveness to do with this event and the all the people involved.

Furthermore, if there is any residue of unforgiveness that I cannot expel on my own, I give permission to the Lord to remove it from my being surgically through His supernatural power.

Having now disposed of this toxic baggage of unforgiveness and turned it over to my Lord and Savior, Christ Jesus, I now pronounce myself free, clear and delivered as of this day forward.

I have decreed this thing and it has been done for me, in the Name of Jesus Christ. Amen.

Signed: _____ Date: _____

Printed Name: _____

Witnessed By: _____

Releasing & Letting Go Contract

Unforgiveness

I, _____, promise my Lord and Savior, Jesus, that as of this date, _____,

I have willingly and deliberately released and let go of all unforgiveness to do with this event and the all the people involved.

Furthermore, if there is any residue of unforgiveness that I cannot expel on my own, I give permission to the Lord to remove it from my being surgically through His supernatural power.

Having now disposed of this toxic baggage of unforgiveness and turned it over to my Lord and Savior, Christ Jesus, I now pronounce myself free, clear and delivered as of this day forward.

I have decreed this thing and it has been done for me, in the Name of Jesus Christ. Amen.

Signed: _____ Date: _____

Printed Name: _____

Witnessed By: _____

Progress Report

Describe how you feel after each session. If there is nothing immediately noticeable, keep a log here from day to day.

Baggage 2
Living In The Past

Baggage 2 -- Living In The Past

This exercise deals with living in the past.

Write down the names of all those who are keeping you held to the past.

Briefly describe the events that caused you to continually look back and live in the past.

Continue on this page …

Concerning this matter, what would you like the Lord to do for you?

Before you let it go forever, is there anything else you'd like to tell the Lord?

Now, turn the page to review the contract.

Don't sign it until the class director says it's time to do so.

Read the Prayer of Acceptance and Deliverance with the class.

Then sign and date both contracts, promising to yourself and to the Lord that you'll never revisit these things again.

Cut out one of the contracts and throw it away – ceremoniously – to commemorate your Day of Deliverance.

If doing this on your own, read the Prayer of Acceptance and Deliverance at the back of this journal and repeat the steps above.

Congratulations on your new-found freedom from living in the past!

Releasing & Letting Go Contract

Living In The Past

I, _____, promise my Lord and Savior, Jesus, that as of this date, _____,

I have willingly and deliberately released and let go of everything to do with this event in the past and the all the people involved.

Furthermore, if there is any residue of looking back that I cannot expel on my own, I give permission to the Lord to remove it from my being surgically through His supernatural power.

Having now disposed of this toxic baggage of living in the past, and turned it over to my Lord and Savior, Christ Jesus, I now pronounce myself free, clear and delivered as of this day forward.

I have decreed this thing and it has been done for me, in the Name of Jesus Christ. Amen.

Signed: _____ Date: _____

Printed Name: _____

Witnessed By: _____

Releasing & Letting Go Contract

Living In The Past

I, _____, promise my Lord and Savior, Jesus, that as of this date, _____,

I have willingly and deliberately released and let go of everything to do with this event in the past and the all the people involved.

Furthermore, if there is any residue of looking back that I cannot expel on my own, I give permission to the Lord to remove it from my being surgically through His supernatural power.

Having now disposed of this toxic baggage of living in the past, and turned it over to my Lord and Savior, Christ Jesus, I now pronounce myself free, clear and delivered as of this day forward.

I have decreed this thing and it has been done for me, in the Name of Jesus Christ. Amen.

Signed: _____ Date: _____

Printed Name: _____

Witnessed By: _____

Progress Report

Describe how you feel after each session. If there is nothing immediately noticeable, keep a log here from day to day.

Baggage 3
Guilt

GUILT!

Baggage 3 -- Guilt

This exercise deals with guilt.

Write down the names of all those who caused you to feel this guilt.

Briefly describe the events that caused you to experience guilt.

Continue on this page …

Concerning this matter, what would you like the Lord to do for you?

Before you let it go forever, is there anything else you'd like to tell the Lord?

Now, turn the page to review the contract.

Don't sign it until the class director says it's time to do so.

Read the Prayer of Acceptance and Deliverance with the class.

Then sign and date both contracts, promising to yourself and to the Lord that you'll never revisit these things again.

Cut out one of the contracts and throw it away – ceremoniously – to commemorate your Day of Deliverance.

If doing this on your own, read the Prayer of Acceptance and Deliverance at the back of this journal and repeat the steps above.

Congratulations on your new-found freedom from guilt!

Releasing & Letting Go Contract

Guilt

I, _____, promise my Lord and Savior, Jesus, that as of this date, _____,

I have willingly and deliberately released my guilt and everything to do with this event and the all the people involved.

Furthermore, if there is any residue of looking back that I cannot expel on my own, I give permission to the Lord to remove it from my being surgically through His supernatural power.

Having now disposed of this toxic baggage of guilt, and turned it over to my Lord and Savior, Christ Jesus, I now pronounce myself free, clear and delivered as of this day forward.

I have decreed this thing and it has been done for me, in the Name of Jesus Christ. Amen.

Signed: _____ Date: _____

Printed Name: _____

Witnessed By: _____

Releasing & Letting Go Contract

Guilt

I, _____, promise my Lord and Savior, Jesus, that as of this date, _____,

I have willingly and deliberately released my guilt and everything to do with this event and the all the people involved.

Furthermore, if there is any residue of looking back that I cannot expel on my own, I give permission to the Lord to remove it from my being surgically through His supernatural power.

Having now disposed of this toxic baggage of guilt, and turned it over to my Lord and Savior, Christ Jesus, I now pronounce myself free, clear and delivered as of this day forward.

I have decreed this thing and it has been done for me, in the Name of Jesus Christ. Amen.

Signed: _____ Date: _____

Printed Name: _____

Witnessed By: _____

Progress Report

Describe how you feel after each session. If there is nothing immediately noticeable, keep a log here from day to day.

Baggage 4
Self-Loathing

SELF/LOATHING

Baggage 4 -- Self-Loathing

This exercise deals with self-loathing, also known as shattered self-esteem.

Write down the names of all those who shattered your self-esteem.

Briefly describe the events that caused you to experience self-loathing.

Continue on this page …

Concerning this matter, what would you like the Lord to do for you?

Before you let it go forever, is there anything else you'd like to tell the Lord?

Now, turn the page to review the contract.

Don't sign it until the class director says it's time to do so.

Read the Prayer of Acceptance and Deliverance with the class.

Then sign and date both contracts, promising to yourself and to the Lord that you'll never revisit these things again.

Cut out one of the contracts and throw it away – ceremoniously – to commemorate your Day of Deliverance.

If doing this on your own, read the Prayer of Acceptance and Deliverance at the back of this journal and repeat the steps above.

Congratulations on your new-found freedom from self-loathing

Releasing & Letting Go Contract
Self-Loathing

I, _____, promise my Lord and Savior, Jesus, that as of this date, _____,

I have willingly and deliberately released my self-loathing, everything to do with this event and the all the people involved.

Furthermore, if there is any residue of looking back that I cannot expel on my own, I give permission to the Lord to remove it from my being surgically through His supernatural power.

Having now disposed of this toxic baggage of self-loathing, and turned it over to my Lord and Savior, Christ Jesus, I now pronounce myself free, clear and delivered as of this day forward.

I have decreed this thing and it has been done for me, in the Name of Jesus Christ. Amen.

Signed: _____ Date: _____

Printed Name: _____

Witnessed By: _____

Releasing & Letting Go Contract

Self-Loathing

I, _____, promise my Lord and Savior, Jesus, that as of this date, _____,

I have willingly and deliberately released my self-loathing, everything to do with this event and the all the people involved.

Furthermore, if there is any residue of looking back that I cannot expel on my own, I give permission to the Lord to remove it from my being surgically through His supernatural power.

Having now disposed of this toxic baggage of self-loathing, and turned it over to my Lord and Savior, Christ Jesus, I now pronounce myself free, clear and delivered as of this day forward.

I have decreed this thing and it has been done for me, in the Name of Jesus Christ. Amen.

Signed: _____ Date: _____

Printed Name: _____

Witnessed By: _____

Progress Report

Describe how you feel after each session. If there is nothing immediately noticeable, keep a log here from day to day.

Baggage 5
Anger / Rage

ANGER / RAGE

Baggage 5 -- Anger / Rage

This exercise deals with anger and rage.

Write down the names of all those who caused you all this anger.

Briefly describe the events that caused you this anger and rage.

Continue on this page ...

Concerning this matter, what would you like the Lord to do for you?

Before you let it go forever, is there anything else you'd like to tell the Lord?

Now, turn the page to review the contract.

Don't sign it until the class director says it's time to do so.

Read the Prayer of Acceptance and Deliverance with the class.

Then sign and date both contracts, promising to yourself and to the Lord that you'll never revisit these things again.

Cut out one of the contracts and throw it away – ceremoniously – to commemorate your Day of Deliverance.

If doing this on your own, read the Prayer of Acceptance and Deliverance at the back of this journal and repeat the steps above.

Congratulations on your new-found freedom from anger and rage!

Releasing & Letting Go Contract

Anger / Rage

I, _____, promise my Lord and Savior, Jesus, that as of this date, _____,

I have willingly and deliberately released my anger and rage and everything to do with this event and the all the people involved.

Furthermore, if there is any residue of looking back that I cannot expel on my own, I give permission to the Lord to remove it from my being surgically through His supernatural power.

Having now disposed of this toxic baggage of anger and rage, and turned it over to my Lord and Savior, Christ Jesus, I now pronounce myself free, clear and delivered as of this day forward.

I have decreed this thing and it has been done for me, in the Name of Jesus Christ. Amen.

Signed: _____ Date: _____

Printed Name: _____

Witnessed By: _____

Releasing & Letting Go Contract
Anger / Rage

I, _____, promise my Lord and Savior, Jesus, that as of this date, _____,

I have willingly and deliberately released my anger and rage and everything to do with this event and the all the people involved.

Furthermore, if there is any residue of looking back that I cannot expel on my own, I give permission to the Lord to remove it from my being surgically through His supernatural power.

Having now disposed of this toxic baggage of anger and rage, and turned it over to my Lord and Savior, Christ Jesus, I now pronounce myself free, clear and delivered as of this day forward.

I have decreed this thing and it has been done for me, in the Name of Jesus Christ. Amen.

Signed: _____ Date: _____

Printed Name: _____

Witnessed By: _____

Progress Report

Describe how you feel after each session. If there is nothing immediately noticeable, keep a log here from day to day.

THE PRAYER

The Prayer of Acceptance And Deliverance

The Prayer of Acceptance & Deliverance

On the next page is the prayer that we will be praying together and come into agreement. It's call *The Prayer of Acceptance and Deliverance* and was given to me by the Lord, especially with you and me in mind.

The prayer will help you to accept, release and let go of those inward/invisible wounds. You are now on your way to total healing and being set free from the bondage of excess baggage.

Let's pray together …

Thank You Father ...

In the Name of Jesus ...

For the gift of your son Jesus. Thank you also for bending your ear low and listening to me. Father, I make these confessions by the words of my mouth, knowing that you will honor my faith, and that you will bring these things to pass. I now confess these things to you:

Father, in the name of Jesus, I refuse to fear any longer. I have no fear because there is no fear in God.

I am not a failure and I am not afraid of what people can do to me. I have faith and trust in you, Lord, to bring me into the purpose, plan, and destiny that you have designed for me. The end has not come yet!

Greater is He who is in me, to cause me to succeed, than he who is in the world, who wants to me to fail.
I am a world overcomer! My faith is the victory that overcomes the world!

I can do all things through Christ who strengthens me. I have the victory and Jesus is His Name. I have it now. I can see it through the eyes of my faith.

Amen ... SO BE IT!

1st John 4:18 says, "There is no fear in love. Perfect love casts out fear… "

The more I release and let go of my pain and broken heart, the more healing and deliverance comes over me.

By casting all my cares and burdens upon you, Lord, you will protect, heal, and deliver me from all my problems.

Lord, you know all the hurts and wounds that I suffered and the many times I have been rejected. You know the things that have been dormant in my inner belly.

Father, by a deliberate act of my will, I lay down and give up all bitterness, resentment, hatred, rejection, abandonment, abuse, my broken heart, unforgiveness and the rebellion that came from those wounds!

I release and let them go now from this day forth, in the Name of Jesus.

*(Now read the names of all those who wounded you.
Read from your sheet of paper)*

I now release myself in forgiveness toward all those who have trespassed against me and wounded me in any way. Help me to do it, Lord! I release the excess baggage that I have held onto. I now let it go and will no longer remember the past.

I now come to you as my Deliverer. Your Word promises in Joel and Romans that whoever calls upon your name shall be delivered. In your name,

Jesus, I ask you to deliver me and set me free from all inward/invisible wounds.

Lord, I release myself from all the power of demonic spirits and I will now walk and live in the full forgiveness of everyone that has ever wounded or rejected me in any way or at any time.

I thank you Lord for setting me free!

I resist and renounce the spirit of rejection, abuse, abandonment, resentment, despair, fear and other sources, and I command them to leave NOW!

I renounce the spirit of inward/invisible and spiritual wounds, and I command them to leave NOW!

Thank you, Father, for the work you have done in me.

My healing will bring great glory to your name and deliverance to many others.

In Jesus' name I pray. Amen.

Your Progress Checklist

So far you have completed the following sessions.

Check the sessions below:

☐   Baggage 1 -- Unforgiveness

☐   Baggage 2 -- Living In The Past

☐   Baggage 3 -- Guilt

☐   Baggage 4 -- Self-Loathing

☐   Baggage 5 -- Anger / Rage

Good work! You did well !

Contact Information

We hope you enjoyed Dr. Patricia Logan-Miles' critical examination of managing inner healing.

To order additional books, go to:

www.HavenofComfort.com

Or write:

Haven of Comfort Ministries

3129 Hacienda Blvd., #365

Hacienda Heights, CA 91745

To schedule a speaking engagement, write:

Email: drpatmiles@yahoo.com

Dr. Logan-Miles' books are also on Amazon:

Search for … Patricia Logan Miles

Made in the USA
Columbia, SC
18 September 2021